LET'S FIND OUT ABOUT

Sikh Gurdwaras

Jane Bingham

www.raintreepublishers.co.uk
Visit our website to find out more information about Raintree books.

To order:
☎ Phone 44 (0) 1865 888112
📄 Send a fax to 44 (0) 1865 314091
💻 Visit the Raintree Bookshop at www.raintreepublishers.co.uk to browse our catalogue and order online.

First published in Great Britain by Raintree, Halley Court, Jordan Hill, Oxford, OX2 8EJ, part of Harcourt Education.
Raintree is a registered trademark of Harcourt Education Ltd.

Editorial: Daniel Nunn and Sarah Chappelow
Design: Ron Kamen and Philippa Baile
Picture research: Hannah Taylor and Sally Claxton
Production: Duncan Gilbert
Religious consultant: Dr Kanwaljit Kaur, British Sikh Education Council

Originated by Modern Age
Printed in China
  by WKT Company Limited

ISBN 1 844 21143 6
10 09 08 07 06
10 9 8 7 6 5 4 3 2 1

British Library Cataloguing in Publication Data
Bingham, Jane
Let's Find Out About Sikh Gurdwaras
   1. Temples, Sikh – Juvenile literature
   2. Sikhism – Customs and practices – Juvenile literature
   I. Title II. Sikh Gurdwaras
   294.6'65
A full catalogue record for this book is available from the British Library.

Acknowledgements
The publishers would like to thank the following for permission to reproduce photographs:

Alamy Images/World Religions Photo Library pp. **12**, **14**, **16**; Arkreligion.com/H. Rogers p. **27**; Christine Osborne p. **23**; Circa Photo Library pp. **6** (Bipin J. Mistry), **13** (John Smith), **19 bottom** (Bipin J. Mistry), **20** (Bipin J. Mistry), **26**; Corbis pp. **4 top** (Bennett Dean/Eye Ubiquitous), **5** (Christine Osborne), **7 top** (Dave Bartruff), **24** (Annie Griffiths Belt); Harjinder Singh Sagoo pp. **4 bottom**, **9**, **10**, **22**; Network Photographers/Denis Doran p. **17**; Photofusion/Format/Judy Harrison pp. **15**, **18**; Sally & Richard Greenhill p. **19 top**; Trip/H. Rogers pp. **7 bottom**, **8**, **21**, **25**.

Cover photograph of the Nanak Sar Sikh Temple in Richmond, British Columbia, Canada, reproduced with permission of Corbis/Gunther Marx Photography.

Every effort has been made to contact copyright holders of any material reproduced in this book. Any omissions will be rectified in subsequent printings if notice is given to the publishers.

The paper used to print this book comes from sustainable resources.

Contents

Words appearing in the text in bold, **like this**, are explained in the Glossary. The Sikh words used in this book are listed with a pronunciation guide on page 29.

What is a gurdwara?

One of the most important gurdwaras is the Golden Temple in Amritsar, India. The first reading of the Guru Granth Sahib took place there.

A gurdwara is a place where Sikhs meet to **worship**. Some gurdwaras are large, beautiful buildings. Others are simple houses, or even just a room. Sikhs can worship anywhere, as long as their **holy** book is there. The Sikh's holy book is called the **Guru Granth Sahib**.

This gurdwara in Birmingham, in the United Kingdom, used to be a row of shops and houses.

Sikhs do not have a fixed day of worship. Gurdwaras are usually open most days a week. However, Sikhs do have a special weekly service. This is often held on a Saturday or Sunday.

A Sikh view

I go to the gurdwara on Sundays, and sometimes for evening prayers in the week. And I have some lessons there. The lessons are quite hard work, but I have lots of fun with my friends.

Satwinder, a Sikh girl living in the United States

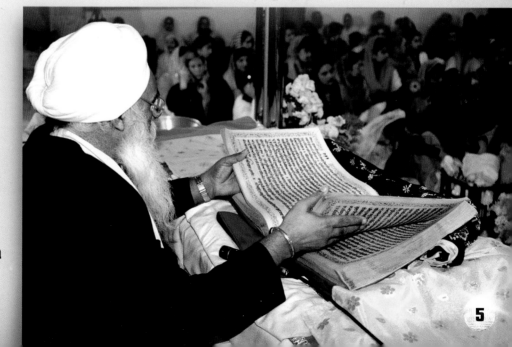

At the heart of every gurdwara is the Guru Granth Sahib.

Sikhs and Sikhism

The Sikh religion began 500 years ago in a part of India known as the Punjab. It was started by a **holy** man called **Guru** Nanak. He taught that there is only one God and that all human beings are equal. This is because they are all equally loved by God.

This picture shows the ten human Gurus. They are grouped around the Sikhs' holy book.

Did you know ?

The word *guru* means "teacher". After Guru Nanak died, there were nine more Gurus. The tenth Guru said there should be no more human teachers. Instead, there would be only the Sikhs' holy book, the **Guru Granth Sahib**.

These Sikhs are performing their duty of sewa by helping out in a gurdwara.

Sikhs believe they must try to help other people. This is called sewa. Sikhs also believe that people may have to live through many different lives before they can finally reach God.

All over the world, Sikhs try to learn **Punjabi**. This is the original language of Sikhism. Services in the gurdwara are usually held in Punjabi.

The Ik Onkar symbol is often found inside a gurdwara. Its letters mean "There is only one God."

Gurdwara buildings

Some gurdwaras are decorated on the outside. Others are very plain. But all gurdwaras have a special flag that flies outside. This flag is known as the nishan sahib.

This gurdwara in India was built to celebrate the life of a Sikh Guru. Most gurdwaras are not as grand as this.

In the centre of the flag is the khanda symbol. This symbol reminds Sikhs that they are entering a **holy** place. Sometimes the khanda is also shown on the walls of a gurdwara.

Every spring, the flagpole is taken down and washed. Then a new flag and wrappings are attached to the pole. This is part of a spring festival known as Baisakhi.

Did you know

The circle on the khanda reminds Sikhs that there is only one God, who has no beginning and no end. The sword in the middle stands for freedom and **justice**. The swords on the outside remind Sikhs to be strong in both their daily life and in their beliefs.

Sikhs put up a fresh nishan sahib flag after the spring ceremony of washing the flagpole.

Inside a gurdwara

Gurdwaras have two main parts. The first part is the **diwan hall**, where Sikhs meet to **worship**. The second is the **langar** hall, where people share a meal after the service. Next to the langar hall is a kitchen where the meal is prepared.

Inside the diwan hall, everyone sits on the floor. They face the **Guru Granth Sahib**, which is raised up on a platform. In some gurdwaras, men sit on one side and women on the other. In others, there is space for whole families to sit together.

Some diwan halls are decorated with tinsel and have pictures on the walls.

Inside the main entrance to the gurdwara, there is a place where people take off their shoes. Larger gurdwaras may also have a classroom, library, offices, and guest rooms where visitors can spend the night.

This diagram shows the layout of a typical gurdwara.

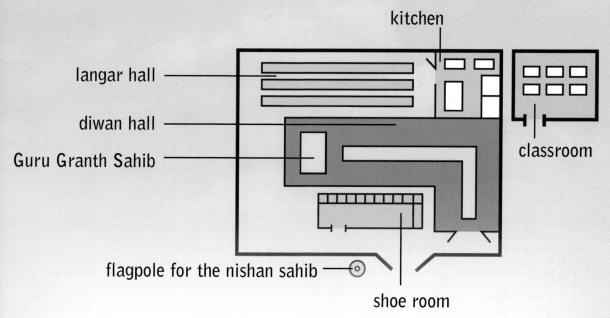

kitchen

langar hall

diwan hall

Guru Granth Sahib

classroom

flagpole for the nishan sahib

shoe room

A Sikh view

When we worship in the diwan hall everyone sits on the floor. It shows that we are all equal in front of God.
Ranjit, a Sikh boy from India

A very special book

The most important part of the gurdwara is the raised platform at the end of the **diwan hall**. This is where the Sikhs' **holy** book, the **Guru Granth Sahib**, is placed.

Sikhs always treat the Guru Granth Sahib with great respect, as if it were a teacher. It rests on cushions and is placed under a **canopy**. During the service, a person known as a **granthi** reads from the holy book. The granthi waves a fan over the book to show respect for its teachings.

A granthi reads from the Guru Granth Sahib and waves a fan over it.

The Guru Granth Sahib is written in poetry. It contains hymns written by the Sikh **Gurus**, as well as by Hindu and Muslim **saints**.

Did you know

In the evenings, there is a service when the Guru Granth Sahib is put away in a special place. In the mornings, the book is brought back to the diwan hall. Carrying the Guru Granth Sahib is a great honour. It is always held above a person's head.

Showing respect

Sikhs must always show respect for their place of **worship**. Being clean is very important, so Sikhs are encouraged to have a bath or shower every day. Before they enter the **diwan hall**, all Sikhs remove their shoes. They also make sure that their heads are covered.

Everybody removes their shoes at the entrance to the gurdwara.

Everyone is expected to treat the **Guru Granth Sahib** with great respect. When Sikhs are seated in the diwan hall, they never allow their feet to point at the **holy** book. This is thought to be rude.

Kesh

Kirpan

Kangha

Kara

Kachera

Many Sikhs wear the Five Ks, which are shown here.

Did you know

Full members of the Sikh religion promise to lead a good life. They wear five symbols to remind them of their promise. The symbols are known as the Five Ks:

- Kesh – uncut hair, often covered by a **turban**
- Kangha – a small wooden comb
- Kirpan – a short sword, to remind Sikhs that they must fight evil
- Kara – a plain steel **bangle**, a symbol of the one God
- Kachera – short trousers, worn as underwear.

Worship in a gurdwara

The aim of Sikh **worship** is to praise God and think about Sikh teachings. People come to the gurdwara to listen to readings from the **Guru Granth Sahib**. They also enjoy kirtan – hymns sung by musicians.

All services end with the ardas, a special prayer that lasts around three to four minutes. Everybody stands with their hands folded while one person leads the prayer. In the first part, Sikhs remember God, the ten **Gurus**, the history of their people, and their beliefs. Then they ask God to watch over people everywhere.

When Sikhs arrive in the gurdwara, they bow to the Guru Granth Sahib. Many people also offer gifts of money or food.

Here, Sikhs are being served with the karah parshad at the end of a service.

To mark the end of the service, small portions of a sweet food called karah parshad are handed out. The sharing of karah parshad shows that everyone is equal in the gurdwara.

Did you know
Some Sikh services can last for up to five hours. Not everyone is expected to stay for the whole time.

People in a gurdwara

There are no **priests** in the Sikh religion. Everyone in the gurdwara has a special role. A person called the **granthi** leads the prayers. Any Sikh who is respected by others can be a granthi.

During the service, someone who has studied the **Guru Granth Sahib** explains passages from the book. The person also gives advice on how to live a good life. This person is called a giani.

A granthi may be a man or a woman, because men and women are equal in the Sikh religion.

The musicians who play their instruments and sing hymns are called **ragis**. Sikhs of all ages can train to be ragis. The people who come to **worship** in the gurdwara are called the sangat.

These ragis are singing hymns and playing the **harmonium** and Indian drums (called tabla).

Did you know

Members of the sangat take turns to do jobs in the gurdwara, such as cleaning and serving food. Anyone who helps like this is called a **sewadar**.

These Indian Sikhs are working as sewadars, washing dishes in a gurdwara.

Sharing a meal

In most langar halls, everyone sits on the floor.

After the weekly service, everyone shares a meal called the **langar**. This is given free to anyone who comes to the gurdwara. This sharing of food is a reminder that all people are equal.

The langar is served in a special room known as the langar hall. Sikhs take turns to work as **sewadars**, cooking and serving the food. The money and food for the langar come from offerings given by people **worshipping** at the gurdwara.

All around the world, the langar is a simple Indian meal. Sikhs are allowed to eat meat, but the food they cook for the langar is always **vegetarian**. This means that anyone can join in their meal.

Langar food is typical of the Punjab area of India, where Sikhism began.

A Sikh view

I like it when it's my family's turn to prepare the langar. It feels good to make food for everyone.

Prakash, a Sikh boy living in the United Kingdom

Special occasions

At certain times of year, Sikhs meet in the gurdwara for special festivals known as gurpurbs. Gurpurbs celebrate the lives of the **Gurus**. They often include a non-stop reading of the **Guru Granth Sahib**. This can take up to 48 hours!

Did you know

For many Sikhs, keeping their hair long is an important part of their religion. Usually, young boys have their hair tied up in a top knot. When they are old enough, they have their first **turban** tied in a special ceremony.

The turban-tying ceremony is a very important day in a young Sikh's life.

Sikhs also meet to mark important family events. Soon after a baby is born, its name is chosen in a naming **ceremony**. The Guru Granth Sahib is opened at any page. Then the first letter on that page becomes the first letter of the baby's name.

During a Sikh marriage, the couple is linked together by a scarf.

In the marriage ceremony, the couple walks around the Guru Granth Sahib, while the **ragis** sing special hymns. When they have walked round four times, they are married.

A place to meet

The gurdwara is not only a place of **worship**. It is also a place where Sikhs can meet up with their friends and family and get to know other Sikhs. They can also learn more about their religion there.

In India, many gurdwaras have rooms for travellers. Some also have clinics for treating sick people. The gurdwara often serves as a social centre for the local Sikh **community**. Music classes, youth clubs, and women's groups may all be held there.

Music classes are often held in the gurdwara.

Many gurdwaras have a classroom where young Sikhs can learn about their religion, beliefs, and history. Here, children are taught to read and write **Punjabi**, the language of Sikhism. Most young people learn how to sing hymns, and some learn to play the **accordion** and the tabla (Indian drums).

Mastering Punjabi is not easy. But once they know the language, Sikhs can take a full part in services.

A Sikh view

I have Punjabi lessons every week, and I learn the tabla – which is great! I'm really looking forward to playing tabla in a service.
Sunita, a Sikh girl living in Canada

Worship at home

Sikhs do not only **worship** in the gurdwara. They also remember God in their daily lives. Every day, Sikhs try to spend some time thinking about God. They may repeat the names for God silently to themselves. This kind of deep thinking is known as **meditating**.

Sikhs try to spend some time meditating every day.

As well as meditating, most Sikhs say special prayers in the mornings and evenings. They also try to read from a **holy** book. Some families have their own copy of the **Guru Granth Sahib**. It is kept in a room of its own and that room becomes a gurdwara.

Other families may have a book of hymns and daily prayers called a gutka. The gutka contains passages taken from the Guru Granth Sahib. Sikhs treat it with great respect.

Did you know ?
Some Sikhs use a mala to help them meditate. This is a prayer rope made up of knots. Sikhs move their fingers along the knots as they pray.

The Sikh boy on the left is reading from a gutka at home.

Sikhism around the world

The Sikh religion began in the Punjab, in India, 500 years ago. Since then, Sikhs have travelled all over the world. Today, there are more than 20 million Sikhs worldwide.

Sikhism is the world's fifth largest religion, after Christianity, Islam, Hinduism, and Buddhism. Sikhs make up 0.4 per cent of the total world population. This means that for every 1,000 people in the world, 4 of them are Sikhs. The greatest number live in India. There are also large Sikh **communities** in the United Kingdom, Canada, and the United States.

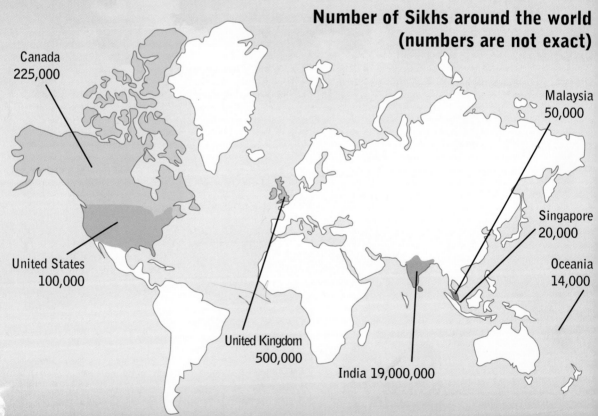

Number of Sikhs around the world (numbers are not exact)

Canada 225,000

Malaysia 50,000

United States 100,000

Singapore 20,000

Oceania 14,000

United Kingdom 500,000

India 19,000,000

Sikh words

These are Sikh words that have been used in this book. You can find out how to say them by reading the pronunciation guide in brackets after each word.

ardas [ar-dars] – prayer said at the end of a Sikh service

Baisakhi [bee-sak-hee] – important Sikh festival celebrated in spring

diwan hall [dee-wan hall] – hall where people meet together to worship

giani [gy-aani] – someone who knows the teachings of the Guru Granth Sahib and can explain them to others

granthi [grun-thee] – someone who reads the Guru Granth Sahib and takes care of it

gurdwara [goor-d-waar-a] – place where the Guru Granth Sahib is kept and Sikhs worship

gurpurb [gur-purb] – a Sikh holy day

Guru [gur-oo] – teacher or holy person. Sikhs follow the teachings of ten Gurus.

Guru Granth Sahib [gur-oo grunth sa-heeb] – the Sikh holy book, which is also seen as a Guru

gutka [goot-ka] – a collection of Sikh hymns

Ik Onkar [ik ong-kar] – the first sentence in the Guru Granth Sahib, meaning "There is only one God."

karah parshad [kur-rar par-shard] – food that is given out to everyone at the end of a Sikh service. Karah parshad is usually a sweet mixture.

khanda [khun-daa] – Sikh sign with a circle and three swords

kirtan [keer-tun] – singing of holy songs

langar [lun-ger] – food that is served to everyone who comes to a gurdwara

mala [maa-la] – knotted rope that many Sikhs use to help them pray

nishan sahib [nish-aan-sa-heeb] – the Sikh flag that is flown outside gurdwaras

ragi [ra-gee] – Sikh musician who sings and plays holy music

sangat [sung-ut] – the people who worship in a gurdwara

sewa [say-va] – the duty of service to others or caring for others

sewadar [say-va-dar] – anyone who performs sewa, the duty of service

tabla [tub-la] – set of two Indian drums. One drum is larger than the other and produces a deeper sound.

Glossary

accordion musical instrument that is played by pressing keys and squeezing a folding box in and out

bangle band worn around the wrist

canopy kind of roof or shade that protects something

ceremony words and actions used to mark a special occasion

community group of people who have things in common

diwan hall hall in a gurdwara where people meet to worship

granthi someone who reads the Guru Granth Sahib and takes care of it

Guru teacher or holy person. Sikhs follow the teachings of ten Gurus.

Guru Granth Sahib the Sikh holy book, which is also seen as a Guru

harmonium musical instrument that is played by pressing keys. A harmonium is like a small organ.

holy to do with God or belonging to God

justice fairness and rightness

langar food that is served to everyone who comes to a gurdwara

meditate think about something very deeply and carefully

priest religious leader who takes services

Punjabi a language spoken by people in the Punjab, an area in north-west India

ragi Sikh musician who sings and plays holy music

saint a holy person, who was very kind and wise

sewadar anyone who performs sewa – the duty of service

turban long strip of cloth that is wrapped around the head to cover it

vegetarian food that does not include meat

worship way of praising and remembering God

Finding out more

Visiting a gurdwara

Sikhs welcome visitors to their gurdwaras, as long as they follow certain rules. Visitors should dress sensibly. When they arrive, they will be asked to remove their shoes and cover their heads. Visitors should always behave respectfully within the gurdwara. In particular, in the diwan hall, they should sit either cross-legged or with their feet pointing away from the holy book.

It is traditional for Sikhs to offer their visitors some food in the dining hall, and visitors should try at least a little. In some gurdwaras, people may be allowed to take photographs, but they should always ask permission first.

More books to read

Celebrations: Baisakhi, Mandy Ross (Heinemann Library, 2001)

Holy Places: The Golden Temple, Vicky Parker (Heinemann Library, 2002)

Religions of the World: Sikhism, Sue Penney (Heinemann Library, 2002)

Useful websites

http://www.bbc.co.uk/religion/religions/sikhism/beliefs/index.shtml
This website from the BBC looks at all aspects of Sikhism.

http://atschool.eduweb.co.uk/carolrb/sikhism/sikhism1.html
This website about Sikhism has been written specially for young people.

Index

Titles in the *Let's Find Out About* series include:

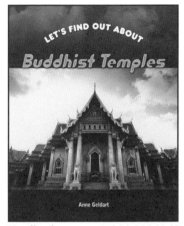

Hardback   1-844-21141-X

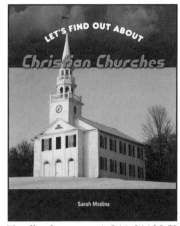

Hardback   1-844-21138-X

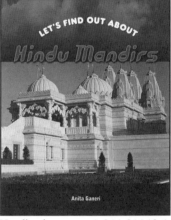

Hardback   1-844-21140-1

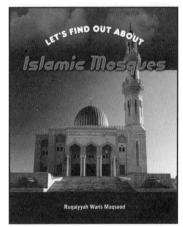

Hardback   1-844-21142-8

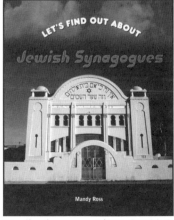

Hardback   1-844-21139-8

Hardback   1-844-21143-6

Find out about other titles from Raintree on our website www.raintreepublishers.co.uk